The Plague Doctor in His Hull-Shaped Hat

THE PLAGUE DOCTOR IN HIS HULL-SHAPED HAT

Stephen Massimilla

AWP
Feb 28 2014

Nathan
Great to meet you at AWP
Best with your writing,
& hope you enjoy these
poems
Stephen
Massimilla

STEPHEN F. AUSTIN STATE UNIVERSITY PRESS

NACOGDOCHES ◆ TEXAS

LIBRARY OF CONGRESS CATALOGING-IN-PUBLICATION DATA
Massimilla, Stephen

The Plague Doctor in His Hull-Shaped Hat / Stephen Massimilla
ISBN: 978-1-62288-007-2

Book design: Laura Davis
Copy editing: Lauren Hawkins
Cover design: Glynnis Osher
Cover art: Stephen Massimilla, drawing on Cecilia R. Mason
        and Atkinson Grimshaw (1836-1893)

Manufactured in the United States of America

Stephen F. Austin State University
PO Box 13007 SFA Station
Nacogdoches, Texas 75962
www.sfasu.edu/sfapress
sfapress@sfasu.edu

Distrubuted by Texas A&M University Consortium
www.tamupress.com

For Sarah Hannah,

in memoriam

CONTENTS

I. HOW FAR I HAD TO GO

II. AN INKY PARABLE

III. NEVER TOUCHED AN OCEAN

[A] feeling normally as individual as the ache of separation from those one loves suddenly became a feeling in which all shared and—together with fear— the greatest affliction of the long period of exile that lay ahead.

—Albert Camus, *The Plague* (1947)

Doctor as yourself.

—Emily Dickinson

I. HOW FAR I HAD TO GO

AT CAPRI

In basil-blue morning lit inwardly
by overlooked light, I wish, O sea—
not quite to live forever, but I do want to take
my fill of you, a long, lascivious look.

Wings list in the wind past
the hydrofoil sluicing airy distance.
Like a wayfarer in porticoed light
who espies the sheen of a nude

lying loose on vanilla pillows, I want to gaze
with the reach of gulls feathering space
over a peach-and-rose sunup glancing
in cold mirrored shells of the Emerald Grotto.

Simmering brilliancies—however touristed—
are like glazes, waves, wicks dipping in a million
minds arriving, sparking, or gone.
Even the most local intimacies

that no visitor ever notices are
requited by the sweep of these waters, stroke
after stroke of mist marking distance,
flour-sack sails, cream-colored coves.

Drifting down past the crusts of cliffs,
fresh breath of lemons, salt, and cypress wood…
Before your conquered and conquering rocks,
my flesh, right here.

Here and forever with empty arms,
any man's ocean-crossing longing.

NOT ENTITLED

I.

I know. By heart I know and do not want
to repeat how I cannot know
all my faces.

Stay with me.

Speak. What to make of walls
when all the doors
fall open?

Lights from leaf-tents of August still feel
their way near, wavering for a welcome
they'll never receive. The room

I longed for won't
recall me. My exile hasn't even begun?

II.

Every day you grow stranger as things
become more familiar. Your hand before my eyes
is like the light

that waves gods away.

III.

Only the window in the mirror holds
our clabbering reflections: You said
we were finished. On my desk,

words not yet spoken by my lips
rewrite the day behind us:

"Old oaks, the house sleeps on."

IV.

Mirrored in the window that backs
your back, a forest of unaccountables
reminds me: You are I, and still

you turn, training yourself, so regained
and cornered, to avoid
moving on. When you leave,

do not say good-bye. Don't ask when
the end will come. Walk away.

AN OVERSIGHT

And there, at the edge of the wash, the salt
spikes of stars spit-
free, I dissolved,
seeing God, or what I thought was, past the veil,
swimmers' limbs   cleaving waves, pliant mirrors.   What has flown

is beyond me. I should have been born

not a man but a flying fish or a feral gull
soaring out over the fish.

I'd be on my way to the next world,
                    a breath glimpsed
        pumping wings

over beaches, frail rigging, parted deeps, *los diablos rojos*—
inner pulse of lights, past the tide

        pulling hard

        through the dark into the next day.

I should have soared.

EVEN *PLEIN-AIR*-ISTS DO/DID MUCH BEHIND AND ON THE INSIDE

Dismembering at its fullest
With no one to hold it:
Unstrung like little Lulu's
Little moony as the morning turns the pages

In Madame La La's bookstall; like all
Parisian bookstalls,
Hers is dark green
Where the bolt was thrown,

Declared to rock doves—
Given to freshest spaces—
Given to between, the leaves
Of tall elms arched over,

Given to Giverny—

Given to be
The gift, the sapphire
Sky and never the down-
Side, but side-by-side in May, may-
Be at the very least the B-

Side to an enclosed garden
In Persia, beryl apples
And topaz lips,

In citrine light of seven o'clock,
Before the river-lover
Is over being novel
And off wheels, rounding and rounding

Before we must give in, give
Up to evening, dress to suit
Level seams, put the big fat
Dog on, foot down,
Teeth sheathed, collar…

Eventually home-yoked,
Or sub or taxi, windshield
Striped with green metal
Bird worry, with what was the sense

Of a future like
The work, the work, the never
Enough getting

Away, remembering the leave,
Pink velvet panache
Flamboyant for a turn for a change.

ARGOS

Ulysses' dog was as faithful as he could be,
given his age and aggressive temperament.
Each year that died, his teeth grew longer; three
or six years more, and the fur went witch. His pent-

up growl was evidenced by the bone he'd gnaw,
then bury, gnaw, then piss near every night
until one day he finally quit. He saw
how pointless faith can be, his master's flight

unexplained by this uncleared bed of dung. Who
could blame the hunter for giving in to sorrow,
invaded by fleas while the suitors swept on through

lodge and lore? The homecoming killed him, or so
the queen presumed. Who can say who sniffs the loom
of love in memory's dismantled room?

STAYING WITH THE MISSISSIPPI

In this riptide of schooling leaves,
                           bone wall dissolves into a great broken vapor
wheel inter-
cut by an overturned cone of light:
                     Snowy egrets unflock, loosen wide
above the cycling mutter, abandon the last sluicing press
of rock to shine on the eyes of the deep, ride up
                          and return to the night.

                         In a moth-fire tide of fliers,
lunatic newsprint, generations have navigated space
in priceless obedience, drawn down-
stream to the cool heel of this bridge
                   where they still stand to cross and get on
with it, maybe not getting this right.
Maybe not, and where everyone crossed, I did. But
                       you sought the river.

HER SACRIFICE

I.

The shaft of darkness extended behind her,
wobbling from rumors in caverns

of the church. Through lenses pitched high
in very old towers, fans turned like daggers;

and the town lay murmuring—a frightened
circus girl, her eyes two trembling

wells of gold. She inched on, though, the old
woman, and shivered on a path

by the shivering lakes (by a rift
in the bleating hills).

II.

By one lake she limped alone, and the geese
raised yellow, leaflike feet

and scattered their steps
as she passed. They peered up behind

dead stumps of rock and birch,
only to shun her and jar themselves in hills

all emerald and beaming with light.
Under their melon-colored beaks,

their chins were doubled like her own,
and they rocked as she rocked

under wings as white and heavy
as her spotted poncho of worsted and frost.

III.

By afternoon her mind was aquiver with feathers
and she could make out only

a waterless landscape
foaming with virgins as plentiful as snowflakes.

She watched them reillumine
all the trees with their nudity as they drew

slowly closer, and the bells of Sunday clustered
in a sky of tender metals.

IV.

Returning home at dusk, she heard trumpets
from the life she had chosen against,

a life of tongues and throaty murmurs,
of geese swallowing the blades

of their reflections, followed by the calm
of the frostbitten moon

trained at nothing, breathing in the fog
like a leopard on an undiscovered peak.

ABOUT SISTER

In lucid moments, she would speak
about lost nights, dungareed vagrant in the outskirts,
dreaming through girders beneath the crust of sidewalk,

waking only when the train stopped at Utica.
Arms signaling in front of her, she would rush along the rat tracks,
blue sheets of newsprint lifting in the heat.

Think back to the vacant house where she cut off
her hair: plaster scraps, blown-rose wallpaper,
folding oak ceilings, and the time

they found her even higher, in a garden on the roof
of a parking garage. Doctor Moses says
this pain leaves you the way she is left:

It never kills. Two months out of the halfway house,
she would hide inside on summer nights, lie
in the sofa's white embrace, searching its arabesque

with her nail. There were no rungs along her arm, her wrist.
But I am sure I knew more: She was the oldest,
platinum hair and a gorgeous complexion.

They said: college, marriage ahead. We would watch
her laughing, smoking, stepping into Saabs,
drawing in her silky leg. I've been searching

a landscape of cut black tunnels and moon-flooded
windows, checking the trash bars and alleyways,
asking. Along a rusty rail beneath a street-level train car

on its side like the carcass of a beast, I find tough, yellow,
cottony flowers twisting from chinks in the tracks, and part
of me urges: *Let me let her go. Let her be.*

VACANCE

Torn moons of your cuticles—
guided by the orbs of your eyes—
found a legless Pekinese in the stone bathroom
as a French cloud went dreaming of your beach chair.
Something moving behind mere passing affection
(white came the star-shoots, white as an old lady's hair),
something behind the sand, your back, your collar-
bone made of air. The old love between us…
I kept thinking
(under the sun's postscript clothesline),
kept thinking one wave
right up
against another…

NEW ENGLAND OEDIPUS

With eyes that debrided sleep,
he'd been the only sound on this side

of New Hampshire, except for
a cough somewhere, the lisp

of a kite in perfect wind, snap
of a stick, what went unsaid.

At home, her ash hairs spread
like tinders, dimmed

L's receding, *skeletal.*
Fall would be thin this year.

This time things would go
listlessly: To side-stepping

chirps of the clock, the woman rocked
through dark until one blind, blood-

scripted eye was opened
and she groaned with surprise.

"Don't," she shushed, to young thumbs
thirling her back, red singe

of her brooch-scratch, sunset
easing her into senselessness.

And as her mistake gave in
to disease, she opened her mouth

and told her last child
(these clinging nerves,

this gossiping chorus of leaves)
how beautiful he was, how much

they had to share: the gin, the sky
all riddled with clouds, everything

coming and going, so little
remaining between.

DUSTY TOOK DIPS

Shot with neon tetras, damsel-
flies, needles, darn them, her skirt
hitched to hurt, never beneath overcoming

footprints in wet surf. But only X-many cubits
from the dunes, nudity, after flesh-colored silk
worn for hours after sundown,

seemed right. Sea unclutching sheets
over pin-striped fish that never come up
in conversation. After each smoothed stretch of my

missed drift, why speak? Next day, all she needed
to catch was her breath, halation lost
to yellow sky in which a salted bride of mist

thinned to trace in branches an alphabet
of the absolute. All along the bleached-
out edge of the fence

the summer after that, she kissed
without reference to ichthyologic acts.
Maybe we were coming up swimmingly,

unfurling among fiddlehead fountains,
forget-me-nots, lit spots dimming
far down the road, in anticipation of the dead

of night in the dead
of summer that followed. Even then, one of us stood
up shaken, torn and fierce as the risen

Lord. Thank God that's over. Now I have to witness
and adjust. Now I have to drive
the goddamn car.

WORRIES ABOUT BEING A WIDOW

Alerted, as Andromache preps cod, by the odor
that flees her notice, her piscivorous pet is ready
for throat-piercing bones. Sea eyes are blood-rimmed.

The skeleton in her loom slips from the back
of the closet, drapes the kitchen clock. Now that she's paid
a penny pretty as her quondam copper midriff for this

unbutterflied iron thing, its breastplate on her counter,
her plan of attack demands a pile-up: ribbons of insides
quick as Circe's chitterlings, soon to be tossed to the cat.

Running for a subway miles from this lopped-off head
and chain mail of fish skin on her thumb, her Hektor
could have his heart attack. A brave man could always fall

through the crowd to the cutting board of dusk. The heart
trapped in her ribs makes her hear his beat. In short,
the distance between what her husband is undergoing on the in-

side and what she is going over in her mind need not be great.
The flesh that connects one heart to the next can be severed
like this strip of fat held captive in her active fist. Any in-

difference to the way things have been heading could give way
any minute. Best to take herself to task, to drill this prep work
deep in neural tissue.

THE UNICORN HAS NO MATCH
OR MATE. THE ARTIST
HAS NO PEER

Getting the world right is a dying operation. To see myself, I swivel
tiny mirrors, piecing each feature together
                                        one suture per second.
In poor sun, I bear witness
                to a scar-pale coat in a small clearing
through skylight shaft, dust of the eglantines sifting about,

plums popping through skins too thin beneath my hooves. Where the Muse
would have posed, I draw her bodice so small.
                It stirrups her breasts; they're lit by interior bulbs. What is that

edging the horn? *My God, it's blood.* She hears the rush
                                        of my head-toss
but won't unfold to feel my snow mane stroke
the neck's arch while
                a man enters wearing—yes, that's it—a pink
surgical mask and whispering to—an assistant?—*This one's*

been killing her foals. Not possible, but yes,
                                the low mound of abdomen
is oozing sap. I know stupidly,

They are here to put down the mare. Her horn gores the ceiling,
but I have yet to draw the eyes.

As the apprentice bends in sky-lit scrubs
to touch a pencil brush,
                I search the set, but the right blue is fly-by-
day. The eyes are huge, tear-pooled, empty of pupils.

Why do I not have the proper blue? In the long run, the draught of truth
cannot not count, as I count to myself,
                        not aloud, only

in my mind, in blank print, the animals said to weep
at the hour of their own dying.

JANUS-GAZING,

two-faced, as we
sphinx-walked

the rickety steps to the beach,
two jays crossed

blue-white beneath
our feet, down

to the bottles
and ruin, the rocks.

Vertigo. Space shook. Sign said,
"Keep Off."

*

Bone-lonely, I'll face back
without me,

fleshless
creaker

in the open no-
where, not

even my fear
to pull close.

ON THE BENEFITS OF A PHILOSOPHY DEGREE

I.

The warmth replaced
with loss becomes part of every other reality,

its appreciation, alive to the touch,
touched every which way, every way.

Not that parting makes us suffer, we're still here
and will be,

in minute shifts, in synaptic buzzing
as blackness hurries wind back to the leaves.

II.

Not thinking of you was a madness,
you know, as not thinking of myself

was the dream of an unbreakable
sleep—I was that broken.

Does the sun shine just because I ask
or because I wanted it to shine because it hurts?

What has already become of me
if something this terrible were to happen.

AT EDGE OF EARTH, VACATING ON THE CHEAP

What comes next? A sky
so buzzard-lovely,
so severe.
Nothing less
than nothing whistling
through the teeth.

Rust of beaches,
mist of vines. Yellowlegs
swizzling S's in air-thin sheets
of surf. Ice-colored nude
is a lizard, a tiny lip twisting beneath
a cyclamen umbrella.

Faint snake of freight train
in the gaps
between canines of cliff-
face, rotted tree stumps lisping: pistil, tower, quarter-
moon of dome. Past pure teeth of foam, raw lips

of sky: Teach me to keep going
nowhere. Please, I have not come
from nowhere just to learn
how not to be scared. There is an end
to never settling for any reaches

of this earth, dream of a precinct
no one can name. With stone eyes that take everything
for granted by blue hunger
that eats at this dwindling spit of cloud-rock
overhead—I want to say (but won't) how far
I had to go to get
this far.

II. AN INKY PARABLE

KORE SETS THE RECORD STRAIGHT

    You pretended to turn crone
before your time, which never comes,

even played the nursemaid
to raise some hero in my place.

    He arrived here fired, dis-
figured. Ears

of millet everywhere
shriveled to sticks, onions

to dirty ember bones. Vole skins
folded upside down

in branches. Others flitted about
like dreams of my first thirteen years,

    when I would watch you
haul the grain into being,

and metal plums and pomegranates,
bumpy leather sacks

of bloodred jellies. I had nightmares
of an iron knife.

    But I had thought:
to unmake me of you,

to strip the bloom and blush
of me, purge

the sap, uproot and fling myself
through the earth

where every leaf and blade
was hateful.

Childish, stupid. I managed it too,
put my tongue to thousand-year-old seeds.

He made me.
Did you think I wouldn't leap

into that chariot the way
a dandelion spur—

your star of ash—
commends itself to wind?

LIFE LINER

Between night and the end,
an unsteady stream
of ultramarine. Sea-stars are

alive, incontestably
numbered. Beard strands
tangle in wave-

rows in my half-opened
eye. Ghoul-fluorescent, a light-
house spotlights

the wing-beats spanning
bridge tower to bridge tower,
terns dipping along the webs

between my fingers, which are
eaten by rust. Clouds touch
the river the Greeks called

Ocean. Horizon oscillates visibly
in mist. Blue blood stains
the passing portholes, a city leaving

a city, blazing its rooms
in a phosphorous wake.
Wash hits the waves.

The waiters aboard
totter trays
of glasses. Swaying

chandeliers. Silver
coins wobble
to no level,

widening dimly.
Constellations
renew their studded

diagrams overhead. How long
have I been
voyaging alone? My heart,

pierced with sky-
holes, spits
and brims over.

METAFORA

The word means to carry from place to place,
not that I can estimate the distance. Love is love
of nothing but *from* to the base of the mountain
where oil and cheeses cool in caves shaded
by cypresses. South Italian cuisine is not all that
metaphoric: You savor the locality of the ingredients,
the secret, the way this sun flashes from your cuticle

into a pure shell of hemisphere, the way this sea
that leans behind your thumb is what the centuries come
after, come over in ships of innumerable sizes, rarely
more than one, a few at a time. The whiff of two flame-
licked sardines or a battered parmesan is enough
to drown out the fleets of Aeneas and Odysseus.

Between this sail in the Bay of Naples and that one,
a speck of volcanic ash in mist, Vesuvius
is speechless. That mountain of shadowy facets lost
its horsetail plume mere decades ago. In the crater:
one burnt-out eye, live stone boiling beneath…

According to Ovid, the Cyclops Polyphemus pre-appeared
south of this region with his vision intact, focused
on a nymph who sent him packing under clouds
that cling to old Sicilian peaks
like sheepish lovers of a tale in which lovers
full of tales recall the way the blind bard originally

retold it. The clouds of Etna shift like sheep grazing
on crusts of shade before the evening meal, morsels
over which to ruminate on how to navigate time
and space. Shades escape the sun's eye by clinging
to fleecy bellies. These vapory signals fore-

shadow the risk of taking (for the tangible feast
and burnt offering) the Cattle of the Sun
that, because they are immortal, live on not *as if*
nothing more, but *as*—if nothing
more than—metaphor.

OCTOPUS IN THE MARKET

I.

I dreamed there was something
dead wrong
with your tongue. Membranes
stretched, a baby bird's gray-pink

questions, it floated polylingually
in your mouth's raw ore.

II.

Tincture of cinnamon
skittering on all eights, the mute
octopus twisted, scribbling
a note that any hope of keeping
your sack of sail on the horizon
was swiveling
from my grasp and slipping down...

(as if holding a pen
from the crate of tentacles,
it had probed past pale rows
of squid
for a crack between stanzas)

to piazza stones,
cart-spawned and wind-wracked
many miles from any outlet
to the ocean...

III.

...until the fisherman recaptured it,
unknotted it in fierce market heat.

Slapped back on the breathing heap,
trembling with wet sepia eyes—
an inky parable.

THE EEL, SIREN

from the icy seas
who shakes off the Baltic
to rejoin our shores, our estuaries, our rivers,
plunging under an opposing
pulse and into another intensity
where life branches, artery to artery,
vein to vein, rooting ever deeper into the heart
of the rock…filtering
though slimy capillaries until, one day,
forked fires striking though the chestnut trees
will ignite a quiver in clots of dead
water trickled from the towering cliffs
of the Apennines to Romagna:
Eel, torchlight, whip,
Cupid's harrow in the earth
which only our mudcracked Pyrenean
gutters can ditch-deliver
to the paradise of fecundity;
green fighting industry, probing
for life where the Rubicon is pulled
into a pillaged underworld;
the spark that says
to make an end is to begin
where everything is charred,
this twig in its grave,
this rainbow, brief twin
to iridescence under your lashes
flashing in the center
of the empire of your eye,
streaming light to the sons of men;
immersed in your bank of mud—in this, can't you
recognize your *sister?*

VESPRO

The two trees in the Garden
of Eden did not bear apples.

Fig leaves on the domes
of your eyes, your lids
crumpling smoke-blue at dawn
reminded me, in half-sleep,
how your breasts from their inward
transformations had reemerged
through your back,
where they doubled
as shoulder blades,
and it was good.

A cool wind chases through the Eternal City.
Were new angels singing at noon?

Viewed from the green peak of the Gianicolo
over bleached grass blades and violet
paving stones, the day-moon
and the dome of St. Peter's
are both eclipsed
by the enormous testicles
of the stone-armored steed
of the mounted Garibaldi,
unifier of Italy.

The moon and the dome of St. Peter's
are pale fluorescing breasts.

When I squint, these sunspots
are areolae the color of split figs.
Your lips are split figs.
We are encrypted in a garden

within the air
behind the air. All of Italy
is ripe and sticky.

TWO IN SICILIAN SUNLIGHT

Guess I'll drop another aspirin moon, he thinks without thinking
he's had too much wine, guzzling a sunset of Sicilian orange, fool's blood,

in fact, on a table of *cioccolata*. Urethra of porcelain teapot hisses
and spies, looking even less likely than she is to be nice. He takes note

(behind his girlfriend's head, they pluck his mental tendons) of teenage *ragazze*
in tight tee-shirts with foreign words like "Freedom" inscribed on them.

With their went-thither hips in zucchini-green denim, they traipse
the *lungomare*, tossing corkscrews of hair. Stylized chaos.

Out of his and her outsiders' observations, a few words flicker
unnervingly, aloud: *So much smoking,* she says.

Living by different rules, he says. Never saw the waiter
serve the fish. The blind eye in its own exploded pus. An hour later,

silver skin and milk-white meat still stringy close to the bone recall
cord-tossed merchandise half-packed in crates. (Like old American military belts

at the Salvation Army, argentine eels had filled the early-dawn gazebos,
button eyes fresh and black and huge. One of them made eye contact

with her.) Cats belonging to no one kept circling, brushing against them,
fangs of ice, tongues given over to delicious luxuries.

NO LONGER A NIGHT GIRL

No longer a night girl whispering
escapades on the S train, she shimmied in black
fishnets, traipsing, instead, the beach.

Pervy bluestocking turned Sicilian
sports black boomerang brows
over ovaline eyes imported from the hotel ceiling.

Lovely enough to bring down a fortress, she arrests
an officer in midstride
outside the Palazzo Publico. As he extends

directions, *Who asked you anyway?* she word-
lessly blurts, a purseless *ragazza* in a string
bikini searching out a lover in the crowd.

On the pigeon-speckled edge of her business,
this cop's just a scrap of piazza
barely jotted by the mix of nerves

behind her contacts. She's an open
book in a language he doesn't speak.
The next man who takes her from behind stands

for love for a quarter-hour on the fringe
of her listening. Like the one who stood
her up, even the cathedral on this street

is in need of an interior answer. A single beam
transfixes the dimness, buckles, and dies
along gold, arched mosaics. On the gold mid-

day beach, the pearly oyster in the velvet crack between her
thighs closed just like any mussel in the cluster
the fisherman was wresting from his big black nets.

SICILIAN SWIFT SPOUTS

I.

Vicious, auspicious reels of *rondini*
in bone-china sky. Glinting,
they come full circle, flit past the window
carrying bits of bugs to fledge-
lings cocooned in grey stucco nests
beneath the eaves. Whirls
of unaccountable rain-birds, micro-
cosmic tempests, pocket gusts
flung up into space, which
comes clear for tiny instances
between spindrift
and smoldering breakers.

Continents dislodged
in the distance stammer
into view, conjuring a ghost race
out of vaporous air. As in the beginning,
lives flicked and fleeing the vortex
scatter their wayfaring songs past
the cave of my ear. No sleep can deafen
those pleas, can subdue that din.
Though I can know nothing much,
there is too much absence here.

II.

In my Sicilian inn nightmares,
forgotten colonies, atrocities,
heart-storms come back poly-
famous, like the rush and crash
of disruptive boulders whose hex-
ameters break before and aft,

rocking me back to the start
of expired surf. My eye
cannot grasp where this crying
arises and dies, cold breaking
into verdigris, the pit of not-
night where tinny lights over waves
collide like comets, silent
to the point of violence.

III.

Recapturing what this journey was like
before I knew where it was
leading, I'm not saying this right.
This ditty could have ended
where it began, entered the watery
door to the dark through which lost
souls spiral—erring, unhearing
and blind to the sun-
rise that fractures
gigantic sea-jaws, mouth
of devouring grinding, voweling
disavowals of renewal.

IV.

Where the sea-wind rises and races
to help feed invisible infants, I'll wake
to the secretive meaning
of vacation. Free of inhuman
or civilized dissent,
germinating angels will yet
uncoil from ashes
for nostrils exulting in salt,
for eyes seeking rain from far countries;

rest assured the whole globe will well
up and dissolve into birds, will roar
and burst in their song.

DESERT RUNES

(Over the Negev)

Engraved in sand-blaze, seething copper. Wobble
closer: Landlocked diagrams spattered with flame
wake dreams of spears and torsos, ancient battles.
"They lived for seven ages." Such is their fame.

Another says, "In the end, they didn't last."
Chains are depicted: miracles, many metals,
ends such as have never been surpassed.
Signs are still taken for wonders. After all,

beyond that ridge, houses flare, molten glass;
and soon, where faint trails end in waves of rock,
a manta's shadow flaps along the surface,
bending over mountains. Tilting back,

we'll soar too far to make this out. Do lies
end up where we can't follow? Even though we
can gaze from as far as they assumed that eyes
could see a meaning too close for them to see?

CONJUGAL SNOWSCAPE WITH SCARECROW

I.

Death is not the way that death defines the things
I list—that gesture, these two sticks—

the way the wind sways some old coat
to scare an unwed bird. Side-prayer is a spider

who gowns a sack
stuffed with straw in forgetting's delirious

script. Make no mistake,
my night, my carbon priest—my love is a blizzard.

Her kisses are black flak,
the end of seeing things too well.

II.

You say this is God?
I am native to this dwindling.

This is a printed list, I tell you,
a burning scented rag doll and an ass.

BREAKTHROUGH

Fyodor's doubt was a door in the cell of his skull.
Wind pried it open. As soon as worry dozed,
any Underground Double could run right through.
Dread, you are vast as the tundras of Russia,

a glacial eye in the keyhole of Peter's port.
I've faced your dead land. Fanged in the blizzard,
another Gogolian gargoyle cracks his fist.
Ergo, I stand mute, smirking like The Idiot.

I lean to let my eyelids bat and burn
as I Nose through a palpitating Cloak of sleet
into night, this Gulag with no stone wall

where the Bronze Horseman wobbles, and I turn.
Now topple my head, Raskolnikov. Let it fall
into a pool of mood, where blood can run to freedom.

GIORGIO'S SAN MARCO

Deserted square at the edge of lightless
tunnels. Zone swept clean of pigeons.
No wings spinning through pinnacles. Only blank

viridian sky, swivel of a street lamp, its shadow dialing
in an arc of gold with no crowd
to stipple it, ripping the ground.

Before we left for Venice, in the gap
between dense violet dreams, I found myself
wandering the night until I found San Marco;

it was like stepping into a jewel cut free of caves
that had kept me hunching forward,
wondering how death would end.

San Marco glittering by water, others
before me walking in a ring from square
to square, staving off interference, looking out

everywhere for gondola collisions,
bottlenecks of crocodiles, thieves
that would abscond with such magnificence.

Dreams were more accurate than the reality.
Even that late in the season, certain cooks
confirmed: Too many shadows,

like aspic labyrinths on dinner plates
after the guests in their jewels had left.
Darkness spreading into vacant space,

Charon poling behind, just out of reach
in the musings of a strolling Surrealist painter,
fluffing birds and flâneurs all gone:

Only charcoal arcades, an empty wheeled cage,
the girl with the hoop running toward
the cut-black statue with his arm stretching out.

APOCALYPTIC SWAN

Swan—your molten neck
flexes like a tube of handblown glass,
Venetian sunset rebirth

where a torch-strewn palace sinks.
You're the flame
of rapture in the loins of Jupiter.

Yes, the ghost of Juliet, the Grace
of suicide, and Nemesis, Cassandra, Rama, Krishna,
death-in-life, an oily slick that plunges

from a heaving tank of crude. Leviathan has
capsized, and the Swan has come up black!
Anhinga, drape us in your wings.

Deliver us from evil. It is midnight;
the plague has struck; the white gourd is rot;
the ancient world is snow-heaped,

our bird poems deep in paper.
All your homeland has to offer
is a crippled aqueduct of swans,

Ledaean echoes paddling past
the wreckage of Parnassus.
You, who split the Cosmos

in the egg white of your eye:
Look to the Pacific for your signet—
white S by an atoll that reeks of iridescent

black. That neck is not your missus's
plunging under, rippling wide. The tail comes up atomic,
buoyed by a trillion feathered cupids. Mister,
won't you take her for your *bride?*

ENTERING VACANT STAGEHANDS

Once she goes to sleep in my script, it is 2:00 A.M.
and she can't get out, will never remember the city

her dreamer has navigated, all by accident. Will return
to his cell, days of flicked sparks in a fireplace

left to rot in Mann's rendition
of hell. The empty moon is a gland

in her neck. And cinched
to the limits of her midriff, her skirt

reveals a Venetian flag tattoo.
Looking better than a girl, a coolly vicious bird

cocks by the lion raging in copper at a liner in the harbor;
the horseman above him swings a saber

at the real moon reflected on kites of newsprint.
The impurity of the street is hitting my belt.

I enter all the unmarked
doors forty feet tall, coffered, browed

with brooding faces of ancient thespians
reflected ill-fittingly in canals—

the wind stripes of night—while that gull
in the fish market still snaps up fish guts,

rips through the newspaper, takes a hop back
from the smell of torture—thumb crusher,

devil's box, beaked stab of the plague doctor
in his hull-shaped hat, and, yes, wild gulls…

It's a tremendous sky that reflects the water,
glitter of mementos desperate for echoes.

Electric stage-wreck in each scavenger's eye,
child after child akimbo

on these pedestals, a longing accordion
of unwanted songs.

LAKESHORE

Jesus, sweetheart, always hauling

a cross I never get: somewhere
you lived
   with an entirely lovely person

capable of catching one
hundred and fifty-
three fishes;

it's all a blur, though, just birds returning
in mist, while
   here you are asking to

recross the lake you already crossed
for so long, so happy to get here;

you can't get across
what no one will understand:

a drying mud valley
is a death of clay, cracked leaves X'd out

like old hands touching fish-junk; terrible facts,
zero impressions of a floor
     that so few and so many once-living once
watched that Someone walking over.

ERASURE

Aroma of ocean oxidizes alloys,
blears nubile to eunuch, softens sunken boards;
the surf withdraws and arrives, leaving its decoys,
the humid beauty of a few stinking forms.

All things, sweetheart, come to nothing real;
by our necks, this faint rope scar rings the land.
But let the children refill the flesh-pink pail,
let waves disfigure the faces they shaped in sand,

weakly mis-taking the measure of models like us.
With rapt, uncalculated motions, they live
on ignorant of the glacial peak glaring at us.

We've lost the art of pretending we'll survive.
There's no breath left that outshines a single breeze
scarcely clearing the patina off this beach.

AUSPEX

Coal-blue cowbird's
on the gutter. Snow or no,

he nods and lollops; he *ack-acks,* angles
his eye, beebee grape

lodged in its socket
of gold. His heart's of home,

of sleep and izzards.
Our bleak psyche blights

the moon, pill "O"
puffed in a cough

of fog, dreams a few leaves
in the chill, holding

on through withered
hands, untrusted sunset

thumbs its rust on willow
root. Windows go

up in flame. Night-spell gropes
for will-o'-

the-wisps, the Who's Who
are holy settling

in, puzzling to unzip
their wizard sleeves. Footprints

fill with sparks
in the bitter drifts that follow,

ahead of them ploughed
with "bull," "moo," and "doze."

Though the dead don't know
what was "I"

could be "Om,"
can a crow climb

the Alp at the end
of the sky, O Zone?

III. NEVER TOUCHED AN OCEAN

THE GUEST AT THE FOOT OF THE BED

as candle, as fur-light, as I lay waking, was staring me down
with cold orchid stones. She must have died

from wanting a human
reply. So much like, so near,

or hosts I don't know spoke
through her: nuns and some cornered by she-hounds,

et al. Her inarticulateness made apology.
It was not her look but a knowledge that she had.

Maybe the wraith I glimpsed autumning
behind her still appears on this earth, as suggested,

where spigots are clicked by pewter leaves
heard fleeing (the neighbor calling from her kitchen door...)

UNI-VERSES

As happenstance happens—just takes

a stance—the verse the writer rights is still as bent

as any object

seen through watery eyes…as darkness

closes in-

doors, where we're safe from gusts of rain,

where candles make moons

of faces, rings around moons, penumbrae

loitering over restless boards

toward the obverse of lateness hanging

on the lake. Between a remembered order and a day

of rendering order, waking to find the writer

writing about

the writer is tiresome: we'd rather leave prodigal autumn

to its falling. The bitterness of wisdom is recalling that even this thought is only what was

written, as if the decision to say it were long or legal, read

or truly rendered.

SACRED DEFOLIATION

after Vallejo

Moon: Crown of an immense head,
You go shedding leaves in gaudy shadows.
Red corona of a Jesus who thinks
Tragically sweet things of emeralds.

Crazed celestial heart,
Why are you rowing like this, inside the cup
Brimming with blue wine, toward the West,
With that ragged, agonized stern?

And gliding away for no reason,
You are holocausted in scattered opals:
You are perhaps my gypsy heart
That wanders in the blue, weeping poems...

FAR-SIGHTED SEER

The twitching nerve of his signature blurred
on a late page of fall, through smoke still coiling
from the pipe he dumped, his head drops back
between volumes. Raccooned in shadow-glasses,

his pupils half hide in these dark woods; and she
in the seat across the desk is bedeviled
by moods obscure to him from even the time
he was her age, she incomprehensibly

Beatrice just then, tied to midriff, smirk
on lips, and something like a dimple in wind
glinting at the edge of her cheek, out there

beyond a leaf-shred captured in the storm glass,
glinting among blue shades of Toussaints that shift
through a riddling of lights on turrets and bridges

behind her, someplace far-gone and never-resolved
and home to the inadmissible imp of a man
who had staked all his vision on nothing but distance.

GLOSS

Nothing binds you to
this garden, to this sky. Blue
shadows swell creeks, plunge

past the sundial. On the verge
of stone nails, a smell of ice
behind the cellar door

which held back your volume
of obligations. In that case,
on that page, one was being

an inch too poetic. Faded,
like shifts of your weight
against my leg. You'd lifted

yourself and left the scrap-
book room, its glossies of wars,
electrical storms: It was not

and did not matter, was time
to leave. The house inched closer, leaned
to follow and eaves-

drop under cover of memorial elm,
murmur of innumerable bees.
The chaise—if it remembered correctly

the dream-fable of the dog
swimming in pools mirrored in windows—
was dismembered in a yard too small

to contain all the emptiness there.
In my still-retrieving hand,
forgetful liquid, your glass

in its last wink.
Blue ink in storage. Still thirsty,
you'd left the gloss of your lip on the rim.

SYNAESTHETIC END OF SUMMER

Summer is like nothing but summer
of salt and primordial soup, of pre-
historic porpoises proposing

                        to surface—
to snort; its syntax clears the mind, reorders it.
The sea fills for the seers whose minds
are nothing to the sea,

                  for materialists,
and for dissolution in visions
as pacific as the sea in which their eyes
swim. To see through

what they look for (the scent of which
only matters or is matter
or *moira* in retrospect) is to know themselves

                        as a hungry gull hovers

ruffled only on the outside over
vermilioning medallions
of jasmine
            rimmed by shadows
                        that mingle to dissipate

lumens of the moon. Tea shades
fade before the harvest
or the moon: aromatic coils

                  of oil, of Sunday, of palm,
                  fugitive shivers
of minnows dimming along
the miniscule breaker
                        by your finger.

In the circuitry of evening,
eel belts return.
                    Evening breaks clear
                              of the mind.

Hot liquid coppers
of seven o'clock
are cloud fleets that mutate
          their infinite way
                    to no end
                              that does not

make us larger. Our shadows reach
back to tropic Abyssinia

in the hypabyssal hour,
                    meteoric sizzle

          on the edge of space
the season has created.

As far as sinking
          indigo eyes
                    of gods,

the tongue by which
the vision is given
                    is but a breath to the gods

as we know them—
our guessed-at horizon
                    compacted of orange

and beet-blood;
the summer of the sun-fed life
of the mind.

HOW TO EAT THE ARTICHOKE

I.

If you gouge,

your unstrategic teeth
cannot penetrate it. Your palate

will reel
like a wronged lover from

the fibrous green;

so you take it
in your hands and pry
edge by edge,

scrape and suck, and lodge
the platinum paste

behind the fortress of your teeth,

and finger open the prickly layers
and flay closer,

toward the core,
toward evening,
opening
inward.

II.

    ...the next minute, the battlement
after that—caution:

scalding oil,
hot ice blossom
                    of garlic
floating in lemon water, a cluster
stripped past delicacy

down to the purple
choke, senses entering into
thistled mystery, dark green

blood-consciousness
        like everything once manifest
        in the market   (excitement in
the hearts   of all the market vegetables,
vegetable-darkness),

artichoke, inner
sanctum that was more than
        the wind   through the thorns,
than lemon,   more
than love   was

no history,   no moment, no offering

                    but parting
in a green night,

        copper crumbs,
                            burnt stars,
asterisks,
        smoke-black pepper.

III.

Let the heart taste loiter
in the bright climb from oblivion,

from the skeletal remnants—
all this junk,

this twitching crackle of dirt, of light.

SPRINGLESS

I suppose I repeat—
I'm already occupied
by hereditary culture,
leaked sepia signature,
secretive weaver's nest.

Everywhere, these revenants,
genes thick as sand,
not receding but overtaking
the lost child.

We are all afraid of the light,
the infant going blind,
wounded in a moment
of parental passion
burning a hole in time,

and for what? So
the torchbearer can enter
into the next agreement,
shed heat on weakness,
expose every pore,
prove me false. So
she can be all right. So
we can go on inheriting
syphilis, neurosis, translation
of the same antimatter. So
what? Loss is recall:
The child also

buries the man.
Chained each to each,
the days go
on, the years, no—

in search of lost ground,
down our carved names
March raindrops plough.

WEDDED

Leaning not facing one
another where the sun
would not enter—
flushed white with hate
could not hear
him heading close—

not afraid for herself
who was so afraid
and growing cold
as the palsied moment
the infant slipped
from its ghostly wrapper—

Sunday morning paper
soaked to the core. War

page withdrew
in shadows of calf boots, bruises
in grass too dark at her feet
to see. A maggot glittered—
earth-delivered till
a delicate thrush broke

over frost, that scissoring
zig, that black scattered flight.

ONCE WINTER

was the out-
line of power, leaning,
once two

flakes, a world
coming near. Once
voles shook and counted

on not remembering how
Siegfried's torso of cold
had been swaying

all winter long. Once winter
weakened, clasped his cane
and quivered,

that furred old presbyter
returned to stony
peaks. A skeleton

of frost
dwindles cryptic
to the stars. Winter

seems so faint. So long, once
the gentleness of rain
is in the wind.

NOTHING AGAINST MODERNISM

In no spaces veined
with ice, hacked by wind—
to be cold as sleep.

In the lifting hint of twilight
through which no Dane
could snarl back,

steam circled
our mugs like bees
around orchids.

One feels a certain
solidarity with someone
claimed by the sorry halo

from the crematorium,
a swirl of gauzy petals
above a spring pool,

sweet ladies. Had she lived,
the prince's mother
would have been

crushed. One feels his eyes
fixed on no head, on vacancy.
Love, vengeance—

the forked stem
of dumb belief
in his brilliant hands.

EXTREME RATIO

The brilliant fascination with which a cat
fixates on a fly;
that's how you held death in your eyes for an instant,
and in your fist, the fraying rope around your life
wasn't enough. You were missing
everything that night,
but you were missing a shade more
than was needed to be no less
than enough.
Now, of life you are left with what's left
and of death you were left a shade.

SELF-PORTRAIT AS A FUCKED AND SKINNY CHICKEN

You uncovered me vine-tangled,
yard-hardened, overgrown.

Now I lie to your face, tarnished.
Janus has painted an oxidant pattern

over the pale cast of my body,
furculum uncracked, cervical vertebrae

intact. To love is to hope to probe?
Mother, can you make yourself feel,

still sealed by a little death, in the crack
where the light in dreams

comes from, a pelvis barely sketched?
Can you make yourself conceive

of fingers, head lolling, top-
heavy under the ribs

you've erected? Hear
the worm and murmur, magma

in the puzzle
of my lungs. From between

your teeth (mixed with cave-
face of moon, wind, and reedy

fumes), moths of the order
Acherontia atropos double-

cross a sparked lump
of candle:

a bit like
but not yet your new life

lost in a clot, a ravel
of blood-colored dust.

SIGNS BY NO LAKE THAT GREEN

I.

Past droplets racing up the wind like insects, voltage
cracked the passage between me
                                    and the mountains.
Geese had been gathering like authors, ruffled dignitaries
                                                at the edge
of the lake, their feet black-rubber-stamping
sand pocked with human knee-prints.
                            A gull cried,
puffed, and plummeted
                        to peck one Canada goose
on the nape. Shivering stripes of life obviously symbolized loss and conflictedness
for an instant.

II.

            Through smoke stripes coiling
                        from the open gas grill,
            I recalled a poet I'd long looked up to, leaning in his white
pin-striped suit pants,
a towel where the white hairs on his nape
stood up around the thin green pool
                        in his collarbone. He must have been thinking his way
                        around lines
                            like these in this poem you are reading
until he came to the part
concerning a dream in which
a goose was quacking about the tranquility
            of the natural landscape, how lightning, in contrast, had once set
            a mattress factory in Brooklyn on fire.

III.

As wide awake then
as I am now, I marveled at how phosphorescent algae
on my fingertips created five firefly lakes.

Like the mirage of a plume
in the poet's quick-blinking hand:
the green tail of a pony that my grandmother once painted
in Brooklyn, back when one
could gallop anywhere.
By that time, the pink, goose-crossed
band of clouds in the sky had spiraled
between the mountains and behind both
his eyes, the caduceus of sentence
and line, mercurial as the gesture with which I wanted him
to ratify my expression, my torn Pumas, even the scribbling goose plumes
I was going to write about. He smiled and signed
the blind air between us,
using a hair-thin lightning charge
as his medium.

MISSED SIGNS

Waiting was always in the nature
of the landscape, merged
with bike lanes, camp roads, similar

signs but signifying differences, boulders
from rock clefts, crushed
pine or bone. Even the far-off face

of mountain was blooded at dawn
by a sudden lake of sun above the lake
of cobalt shagged with shade. More sun

broke perilously close, on fawn
and doe browsing in spun mist. Looking
out, we stopped

breathing, never to share a slow climb
to the slippery bottom
of that great glass eye again.

      All I'd have taken away
scalds like love no longer
bound to live, reflection of my own

impatience in eyes that glanced
and were gone. Looking down, you wavered
to warn you would not go

swimming where our yellow figures, or none
or few, still hung
like sun-sparked flies

over the lake. You always made your living
staying alive. The doe about to bound
into the road was always posted on its sign.

ENTR'ACTE

I.

You, the artist, were the meaning
of what you performed. Of this I am sure
though I am not sure

that you can survive your talents.
Were they the living costumes you've cast
fraying into night? Have you wandered

from the landscapes that kill?
Has the rebel been extinguished
in the arms of his treacherous gifts,

which now lie clean-pressed in the annals
of Nessus? Sure, you are perfect, free of torture,
Prometheus drawing his garnet flesh

from the rock, climbing
freely to where the ocean breaks, too deeply
torn, too wise for musty pleasure,

but also too emptied
of blood to cry out...among old leather
knife boxes, scarred, but empty.

II.

A heroine in pain is someday lifted
from that spot, while in the scarlet ocean
the Kraken gropes and coils. Then in the mountains,

a child is born, his voice quick to stress
his quiet needs. With hot-blooded hands, he strangles
cold snakes. He will robe his body in the skin of a lion.

III.

Ages later, from the skull of your theater,
You'll claim to glimpse him—half man,
half myth—hissing through the pulpous night

over vacant airport fields, with one more
rage of spiders
spreading through his brain.

TROPIC TROPING BIRD

My world is each changeling
stroke, a god's

blue breath. Where clutches end,
nothing much to grasp.

My skin shines
like melted pennies.

That's how the light is on watch.
Eternity is incremental. A mouth-

to-trough existence is simple.
Our regard for each other a series

of seconds raring
to stare and stare. Narcissistic?

Not for me to say. All is blood gain,
fib by fib. I wonder, hot-bladed "loon,"

are you one such bit of marginalia,
a pattern of foxfire scat strewn

wherever I turn? Love of pleasure wakes
you, copper-steeped

in peacock virtues, puffed
and startled with disgust.

THE QUEST OF YOUTH IS YELLOW

Nature rarer uses Yellow
—Emily Dickinson

In the poor south
before a storm, when sky turns yellow,
terribly yellow,
and the bee-home turns bright
and bees burn in,
I love the whiffs of honeysuckle,
the buzz in the mimosa.

The quest of youth is yellow,
low in the dawn
or drawn in the dark,
like a flash of that sword
the knight freed from the stone.
On a ride through the English countryside,
blinking past fields of oilseed rape,
I want to live out a day that will blaze
into yellow. Speed rips up tracks, and fields
reel on, like California sand
to bicycles of lemon rind:

O peel back your golden thighs
along the yellow Squaw Valley roads!
Topaz eyes of horses stalled in grassy waves
of flame make me want to double-
cross the double yellow line.
From Santa Monica to Montpelier,
all the traffic lights switch yellow
even in the dead of winter,
but to be elsewhere:

Yellow fish and lizards, yellow crowns
of cockatiels. Leafy seahorses are yellow
in the Philippines. Never mind jaundice or wasps.
Think butterflies, banana pies, four and twenty
blackbirds' beaks, sweetest part
of the pineapple, but to be arbitrary:
saffron pistils, tiger's eyes.

And in the Hagia Sophia, priceless in rays
of the eggshell domes,
a small plain bowl,
most buttery of all the sultan's treasure,
Byzantine perfection of its glaze:
yellow from the fire, phoenix in the gyre,
mixing bowl for ocher,
pastry dough, chickee-fluff, yolk.
O life, luster, halo, joy:
Be the Color-Meister of my soul!

TIME

In the dream of the absolute
to which

to fall,
I believe

you smiled with your eyes
shut.

Fury of night, throw
the big thing out there, a revelation…

There
can be none.

All my life I misunderstood
pain, wandered in a maze

of urban noise.
Never touched an ocean.

BLUE MEDINA

O far-off lot of camels scratching your rock-rears on cork trees,
from sodium foothills to the fistula
some missionary called a river:
To speak of it is to gut it,
but this life's no garden of forking paths.

Children run the gutters like shadow-cats,
slashes of intangible ash under skies
impaled on minarets. Muezzin cry comes straight
out of Africa, but not I, trailing in mazy motions
of the desert past noon, hooked on a glint
of sheep gut to this last buckling
three-legged donkey.

Dusked in drought, parapet ruins sink
to window-pitted, windless limits, adjectival, il-
literate as teeth. Nobody's words. Nobody's market.

If there is a day-moon, it is choked in the throat
of an old Berber beggar, his arms pricked
with sprigs of rosemary, obsession treated
with thick-veined goat meat.

If, through flame-portals framed
in bone stencil, I love Imamu past ebony, past death, she is iliac-
crested, isomagnetic. All attempts to touch anything fresher

are white digitalis on apothecary sills
lined with dying light, powder burns,
these tracers, these too-
distant birds. Dust-quick, blood-
thirsty, earlier than
darkness, they're necromantic.

UPĀDĀNA

I envy the victim
bloated under
water, born
filtering light

through open eyes. If I die, did I see
to the killing? Now do blue
pupils shine fugitive

through lids closed
too late? You wouldn't draw them
for me,

blindly as I reached
for black sky, cool lunation
filtering through like water

from an elephant tank, leaving me
this freshness.
Virescent metal bird—

whatever stripes my mind—
to name you, to shoot you
is to falsify

your cry. No one, good God,
is India.
Next dark noon, I'll let
go of gods.

UNENTITLED

I know I repeat. By heart I repeat and shall not want.
Here we are again in a circle,
a heavy gaze—like rope—

above our heads
and clouds of loitering quiet.
Only the mirror of a mirror holds

our clabbering reflections, a god
half-revealed on my lips.
And one of we—it is

I—has fallen in love. A winged beast
lights that cliff-face,
and I am simple, like this tree.

And the second of we—it is also I—has instigated
blood price for hate. A blade
flashing from these eyes is not worth

its salt-drip of trembling. And the third—
I, I, I—reflecting these, felt his eyes
burst. A blank face of a cloud moves

over the deep. And the last is the one I
know, who should have loved the faces
turned to meet the face they met,

who turns aside to face the route
that runs too late.
And this face, very sick and close

to life, before me
watches faces die in lilac waves
toward August

and shall not want.

ETYMOLOGY

Out of yellow brain, out
of ear, through the wheat
spear in the eye, at

least the window, over
cities, ranges,
ocean, but

I don't mean
a letting go
of some circus

maximus,
a brutal
parent, disease.

I mean more
than consuming
with blue teeth

of flame,
or even love, more a felt
relinquishing,

as when sky gives in
to bird
or the black

trunk of oak caves
to encroaching moss
or the swan slips

a valley of light
beneath its beak,
as the river tears

its skin
to accept a stray branch.
I feel that way

when I release me
to worlds
I can't under-

stand, and
I stand, wanting
air in my blood

and its nostalgia,
Latin
for our pain.

NOTES

AT CAPRI

"conquered and conquering rocks": Capri played an important role in the political and military history of ancient Rome. Octavian and later Tiberius directed the empire from there. Tiberius invited Caligula, his eventual successor, to join him at Capri. In the Middle Ages, the island underwent invasions by the Saracens, and the local population hid out in the grottos. Invasions continued throughout the Renaissance. In the seventeenth century, Capri was hit by the Plague. The island was a site of fierce conflict during the Napoleonic period. The nineteenth Century saw Bohemian and royal tourist invasions, followed by latter-day tourism, part-and-parcel of some of the "local intimacies."

AN OVERSIGHT

Los diablos rojos (Spanish for "the red devils") are the Humboldt squid *(Dosidicus gigas)*, also known as "jumbo flying squid": large, predatory deep-water creatures. They can change their skin color from greenish-white to red (like aquatic traffic signals) and have been sighted near the surface from the Tierra del Fuego to Alaska. Each has tentacles lined with sharp teeth; with these, it grips prey and drags it toward a beak that can easily lacerate human flesh. "The Red Devils" also refers to numerous parachute regiments, fighter squadrons, infantry teams, and teams of acrobats.

EVEN *PLEIN-AIR*-ISTS DO/DID MUCH BEHIND AND ON THE INSIDE

plein air: pertaining to outdoor painting in natural light, an approach first popularized in the 1870s in France.

"Giverny": the famous French county division, site of the house, water garden, and flower garden of Impressionist painter Claude Monet.

"enclosed garden": the root meaning, in the Eastern Old Iranian language, to which the English word "paradise" can ultimately be traced.

ARGOS

See the *Odyssey*, Book XVII.

This poem owes something to Nemo.

NEW ENGLAND OEDIPUS

"mistake gave in / to disease": Sophocles' tragedy is haunted by references to the plague of Thebes (which may well have been inspired by the historical plague of Athens that Thucydides also describes). The expulsion of the "pollution" and the eventual end of the epidemic defines an alleged return *(nostos)* to the *status quo ante*. Still, in an older version of the myth presented in the *Odyssey,* Book XI, Oedipus is not expelled from Thebes.

WORRIES ABOUT BEING A WIDOW
See the *Iliad,* Book VI.

The etymological meaning of the name "Andromache" could be "man-battler" or "man-killer," as well as "[she] whose husband excels in battle."

"unbutterflied iron thing": Today it is common to purchase cod in filets. It takes fortitude to tackle the entire fish.

THE UNICORN HAS NO MATCH / OR MATE. THE ARTIST / HAS NO PEER
For the original lineation and context of the title, see William Carlos Williams's *Paterson* (New York: New Directions, 1995), p. 209.

This poem owes a lot to E. Rotterman.

JANUS-GAZING
Janus, the Roman god of gates, doors, time, transitions, and endings, is "two-faced": He looks simultaneously to the future and the past. The month of January was named after him.

AT EDGE OF EARTH, VACATING ON THE CHEAP
The alternate title of this poem is "Talisman, Prayer."

The yellowlegs leaves distinct tracks. Among the greater yellowlegs, it is only a very rare vagrant that makes its way from the New World to Western Europe (though, oddly, the lesser yellowlegs has been known to winter in Great Britain).

A cyclamen is a wild Old World perennial. The ancient Greek root of the word means "circle." (The word "cyclamen" also mysteriously contains the words "cycle," "men," and "amen.")

KORE SETS THE RECORD STRAIGHT
Though Ovid and others offer various accounts (of why she consumed the pomegranate seeds, for instance), Persephone's perspective—even as presented in *Hymn to Demeter,* the oldest recorded version of the myth—is a matter of speculation.

LIFE LINER
The Titan Oceanus was often represented as a man with a long beard. He tended to hover outside the conflicts that marked the history of the unstable world he girded.

METAFORA

From Latin *metaphora*, from ancient Greek *meta* ("across, between") + *phero* ("to carry").

According to one tradition, Hercules was *on his way* to Sicily in the performance of his labors when he subdued the giants in the region of Vesuvius (which is still a dangerous volcano).

The word "Cyclops" contains a root meaning "cycle," and "Polyphemus" means "many-famed" or "many-voiced" in Homeric Greek. See the *Odyssey*, Book IX and Pseudo-Apollodorus, *Bibliotheca*, E 7.3–9.

For the later Polyphemus and Galatea tale, see Ovid, *Metamorphoses*, Book XIII: 738–897 and Theocritus, *Idylls* VI and XI. (Galatea's lover became a river that flowed past Etna.)

For the Cattle of the Sun episode, see the *Odyssey*, Book XII. According to Odysseus, when his men attempted to eat the cows, the meat lowed on the spits and the skins crawled on the ground. The cattle of Helios can never die, not even when they are consumed.

Virgil's glimpse at the Cyclops in the *Aeneid*, Book III is also intriguing; and in Book VIII, following Euripides and others, Virgil identifies Mount Etna in Sicily as the volcanic vent deep beneath which the Cyclopean smithies forge the tools of the gods. (Etna was itself allegedly named after the nymph Aetna, who arbitrated the possession of Sicily.)

THE EEL, SIREN

Loosely after Montale, whose redemptive eel — our Darwinian relative— overcomes the Alps, earthly despair, and perhaps the aftermath of World War II, but not the modern ecological crisis.

Today, Svignano sul Rubicone is an industrial town; the Rubicon has become one of the most polluted and diminished rivers in Romagna, practically eliminated by the exploitation of groundwater.

In his poems, Montale uses the word *iride* to mean not just the iris of the eye but also a rainbow, iridescence, the messenger of the gods, and the flower. Here I avoid using the word "iris" altogether.

Montale refers neither to an "empire" nor to the Rubicon, but his hero, Dante, believed that an earthly paradise modeled on the alleged unity of ancient Rome could pave the way for the New Jerusalem. (Dante equates Cassius and Brutus with Judas for betraying Caesar; and in the *Paradiso*, the Pilgrim meets the Emperor Justinian of Nova Roma. Dante's Anchises-like ancestor, Cacciaguida, later tells him that his poetry will help heal an ailing world.)

VESPRO

The title refers to an evening song (and a service that included the office of Vespers).

The Gianicolo or Janiculum is one of the highest hills of Rome. It was named after the god Janus, who looks forward and back; he was allegedly worshipped there in ancient times. (See the note to "Janus-Gazing.")

An equestrian statue of Garibaldi, who on this hill fought French troops summoned by Pope Pius IX, stands at the center of the piazza; and a little below sits a cannon that fires blank shells every day at noon and can be heard all the way to the Coliseum. The practice was instated by Pope Pius IX to help coordinate all the church bells of Rome.

SICILIAN SWIFT SPOUTS

Dante seems to have based his depiction of lustful, out-of-control sinners swirling in the never-ceasing storm in Canto V of the *Inferno* on his observation of birds like these, though he speaks not of fleet, agile swifts but of starlings, which likewise band together in huge numbers and black out the sky.

Section II alludes to Odysseus' confrontation with Polyphemus in the *Odyssey*, Book IX. (Also see the note to the poem *"Metafora."*)

The term "verdigris" can refer to the green patina formed when bronze is weathered by exposure to seawater. The etymological meaning of the word is "green of Greece" since artists in ancient Greece relied on verdigris pigment—to paint Odyssean scenes, for instance.

In section IV, I think I was thinking of Sassoon's line "Everyone suddenly burst out singing" and Prospero's speech in *The Tempest*, Act IV, sc. i ("Ye all which it inherit, shall dissolve," etc.), along with Psalm 98 and others that stress that—though it has been witness to all human folly—when redemption comes, the sea will roar with joy. Of course, Sassoon's "Everyone Sang" and the Psalms in question convey different outlooks.

DESERT RUNES

There are many ways to read the runes. The cities of Haluza (Halasa, Elusa), Mamshit, Avdat, and Shivta, along with vestiges of associated fortresses, sophisticated irrigation systems, forts, and caravanserai, are spread along the ancient incense and spice routes leading to the Mediterranean. Many inscriptions have been discovered there. Historic periods and peoples who settled the Negev desert are sometimes identified as Nomadic (including Canaanite settlements), Biblical (Abraham allegedly lived there, and later the Tribe of Judah), Nabataean, Roman, Byzantine, Early Islamic, and Bedouin.

BREAKTHROUGH

Works referenced, often by means of capitalized words, include Gogol's stories "The Cloak" and "The Nose," Pushkin's long poem *The Bronze Horseman*, Solzhenitsyn's novel *The Gulag Archipelago*, and Dostoevsky's novels *The Idiot* and *Crime and Punishment*.

GIORGIO'S SAN MARCO

The title refers to the Surrealist painter Giorgio de Chirico. This poem owes a lot to Sarah.

APOCALYPTIC SWAN

See "The Eel, Siren."

"Rama, Krishna": Upon witnessing the first atomic blast south of Los Alamos, Robert Oppenheimer famously recalled Krishna's revelation to Arjuna in the Eleventh Teaching of the Bhagavad-Gita: "I am become death, destroyer of worlds." Krishna leads up to this revelation by appearing in many incarnations in the Tenth Teaching.

Leviathan is here envisioned as an oil tanker. The term "Leviathan" derives from a Hebrew word meaning "great water beast." A Biblical embodiment of evil, it is probably related to Tiamat, the Near Eastern monster of primal chaos. (*Tehom*, the Hebrew word for the "deep" in Genesis, may be cognate with "Tiamat.")

"anhinga": snakebird or water turkey; in the Brazilian Tupi language, "devil bird." The anhinga does not have an oily water-resistant feather coating and must spread its wings to dry them. But it looks oily.

The white gourd is a melon, also known as the "winter melon."

"Signet" is a homophone for "cygnet."

"atoll": Bikini Atoll, site of many atomic bomb tests of the 1940s and 1950s.

ENTERING VACANT STAGEHANDS

The plague doctor mask—the beak, hood and hat—was conceived as a primitive gas mask. The beak was stuffed with herbs and flowers to block out unpleasant odors mistakenly believed to be the principal cause of disease. The full costume, including the jacket and gloves, actually did help protect doctors against infected fleas. The commercial prosperity of the Venetian Republic as a trading power led to the influx of the rats and fleas that spread the Black Death, which sent the empire on a downward spiral culminating in its defeat by the Ottoman Turks and later Napoleon.

Today, given that tourism has been its principal industry since the nineteenth century, the city of Venice is at risk of dying in another sense and becoming little more than a museum.

In *Death in Venice*, the encroaching plague that Mann portrays is a cholera epidemic, though Mann is making a psychosociological critique.

LAKESHORE

See Luke 5:1–11 for the miraculous catch of 153 fishes (or see John 21:1–24, where it takes place after the Resurrection). 153 is a significant number, as the Gospels are all music and no noise.

The account of Jesus walking on water is "missing" from Luke.

AUSPEX

"beebee grape": BB grapeshot.

An "auspex" (the word shares roots with such terms as "auspicious" and "haruspicy") is an ancient Roman augur whose interpretation of omens derived from his observation of birds.

The cowbird is a brood parasitic New World bird. The brown-headed cowbird has bluish plumage and forages on the ground, often following grazing animals such as cows. It heads south in winter and does not often encounter snow. The crow is of an entirely different species and is now considered to be among the world's most intelligent animals.

Om is a mystical Sanskrit sound, one of the most popular and sacred mantras in various Hindu, Buddhist, and Jainist traditions. The Mandukya Upanishad is devoted entirely to exploring the meaning of this syllable, which can be said phonologically to symbolize the cycle of Brahma, Vishnu, and Shiva (the beginning, duration, and end of the universe). "Om" can be interpreted as the name of God and can be translated as "I Am."

SACRED DEFOLIATION

Since *Los Heraldos Negros* was written in 1918 and César Vallejo died in 1938, he could not have intended his verb *holocaustarse ("te holocaustas")* to remind us of the Holocaust. It is now impossible to read this word in a poem without making that association.

FAR-SIGHTED SEER

Toussaints or All Saints Day, between Halloween and All Soul's Day, commemorates those who have achieved a beatific vision in Heaven.

GLOSS

See J. V. Cunningham's short poem "To the Reader" for an apt gloss on this note to "Gloss."

SYNAESTHETIC END OF SUMMER

moira: one's secretly allotted portion or share; or, from the Homeric Greek perspective, that which in hindsight was destined to be.

"hypabyssal": subvulcanic; pertaining to igneous rock with an almost plutonic texture, originating at medium to shallow depths within the earth's crust. Though it contains the root "abyssal," the word bears no technical relation to oceanic abysses.

"indigo": At the same time that the British East India Company was importing indigo dye from India (the oldest center for indigo dyeing and the source of the Greek root of the word), Sir Isaac Newton introduced it as a spectral color. The distinguishability of this hue has been disputed ever since. Oliver Sacks claims to have seen it during a drug-induced hallucination episode.

HOW TO EAT THE ARTICHOKE
Part of this poem was possibly inspired by Neruda.

NOTHING AGAINST MODERNISM
"sweet ladies": The words "Good night, ladies; good night, sweet ladies; good night, good night" conclude Ophelia's final speech in *Hamlet*, Act IV, sc. v (words which T. S. Eliot echoes at the conclusion to Part II of *The Waste Land*).

"on vacancy": In Act III, sc. iv, Gertrude asks Hamlet, "Alas, how is't with you, / That you do bend your eye on vacancy."

EXTREME RATIO
Very loosely after Cuneo, the Chilean critic and poet.

In Book VI, Proposition XXX of his *Elements*, Euclid explains how to cut a line "in mean and extreme ratio": that is—how to find the golden section point on a line, where the ratio of the shorter part of the line to the greater part is the same as the ratio of the greater part to the whole line. What Euclid called dividing a line "in mean and extreme ratio" gave rise to such phrases as "golden mean," "golden ratio," and "divine proportion." The term "extreme ratio" does not normally appear without the term "mean." The similar-looking term "ultimate ratio" refers to the limiting value of a ratio, that toward which a series tends, but which it cannot pass.

SELF-PORTRAIT AS A FUCKED AND SKINNY CHICKEN
"furculum": wishbone, merrythought. Still, the word "chicken" in this title is not to be taken literally.

Acherontia atropos: the Death's-head Hawk moth, notorious for the skull-shaped marking on its thorax. The genus name *Acherontia* refers to Acheron, the river of woe (*achos, akhos,* the root of the English word "ache") in the mythic Greek underworld. The species name *Atropos* means "unbending" or "not to be turned." *Atropos* is also one of the three *Moirai* or Fates, specifically the one who cuts the thread of life.

MISSED SIGNS
This poem uses Dante's *Commedia* as a subtext.

ENTR'ACTE

Prometheus can be regarded as a culture hero. He stole fire for human use, enabling civilization. The Romantics associated him with the rebel artist (as well as with Milton's Satan, Christ, *et al.*). Though Zeus condemned Prometheus to eternal eagle-inflicted torture, he was in some accounts (including that in the Greek tragedy *Prometheus Bound*) eventually freed by the younger hero Heracles. Perseus, a much older culture hero, was the ancestor of Heracles. Perseus rescued Andromache from Cetus, here figured as the Kraken, the many-armed sea monster known for its enormousness and enormity. Tennyson associated this Norwegian monster with the dragon of the Apocalypse, and a very strong black rum from the Caribbean was named after it.

Heracles wore the pelt of the Nemean lion; his first labor had been to slay it. Nessus was the centaur whose poison blood led to Heracles' undoing. Never imagining that the deadly toxin could come back to haunt him, Heracles had tipped an arrow with the blood of the Hydra (from his second labor) and shot Nessus with it to prevent him from abducting Deïaneira. Deceived by the dying Nessus into believing it was a love potion, Deïaneira laced a tunic with the centaur's tainted blood and later presented it to Heracles. When he put it on, he burned with so much agony that he threw himself on his own pyre. Heracles was known for his fits of rage. Accounts of his death are inconsistent: He is the only hero in Greek mythology to prove simultaneously mortal and immortal. When he died, his spirit descended to the underworld, and Zeus at that same moment immortalized him, perhaps.

THE QUEST OF YOUTH IS YELLOW

"Be the Color-Meister of my soul": See W. B. Yeats, "Sailing to Byzantium."

BLUE MEDINA

A fistula is a passageway between organs that are not ordinarily connected (often a pathological condition).

Rosemary has been shown to prevent blood clots, and it has many other medicinal uses, though few have been studied scientifically.

"Imamu" is a beautiful African name meaning "spiritual leader" in Swahili. It is related to the name "Iman," which means "faith" in Arabic.

The iliac crest edges the wing of the pelvis; it contains a lot of red bone marrow. "Iliac" and "lilac" are almost anagrams.

The term "isomagnetic" refers to lines that connect points of equal magnetic induction or intensity. (An "isomagnetic disintegrator" is a science fiction weapon.)

Digitalis can be used effectively to treat heart conditions and save lives. Still, because of its potentially toxic effects on the heart, stomach, and brain, it has been called "dead man's bells" and "witch's gloves." It can also cause xanthopsia (yellow or jaundiced vision) or visual halos.

UPĀDĀNA

The title of this poem means "attachment" in Sanskrit and Pali. It is the *letting go*, the cessation of *upādāna*, that leads to *Nirvana*.

UNENTITLED

Very loosely after Baczynski (1921–1944).
Yes, it is technically verboten to say "of we."

ACKNOWLEDGMENTS

Grateful acknowledgment is made to the editors and readers of the following publications, in which these poems have appeared, often in earlier versions:

AGNI: "Missed Signs"
Alabama Literary Review: "Far-Sighted Seer"
Argestes: "Entr'acte," "Sacred Defoliation"
Assisi: "An Oversight"
Atlanta Review: "At Capri"
Barrow Street: "The Guest at the Foot of the Bed"
Big City Lit: "At Capri," "The Quest of Youth Is Yellow" (reprints)
Bluestem: "Once Winter," *"Vespro"*
The Cape Rock: "Desert Runes," "How to Eat the Artichoke" (reprint)
The Chaffin Journal: "Auspex"
Chelsea: "Self-Portrait as a Fucked and Skinny Chicken"
DecomP: "Dusty Took Dips"
Denver Quarterly: "Entering Vacant Stagehands"
Drumvoices Review: "Far-Sighted Seer" (reprint)
Eleven Eleven: "Erasure"
Folio: "Kore Sets the Record Straight"
Fourteen Hills: "The Unicorn Has No Match / Or Mate. The Artist / Has No Peer"
Fulcrum: "Uni-Verses"
The Greensboro Review: "Etymology"
The Grey Sparrow: "Octopus in the Market," "Lakeshore"
Hubbub: "Worries about Being a Widow"
Hunger Mountain: "Unentitled"
InDigest: "Gloss"
The Laurel Review: "Even *Plein Air*-ists Do/Did Much Behind and on the Inside," "Extreme Ratio"
The Literary Review: "Her Sacrifice"
Mead: The Magazine of Literature and Libations: "Janus-Gazing," "Two in Sicilian Sunlight"
Minetta Review: "Not Entitled"
Minnetonka Review: "Giorgio's San Marco," "No Longer a Night Girl," "The Quest of Youth Is Yellow"
Nashville Review: "Tropic Troping Bird"
Natural Bridge: "About Sister"
New Delta Review: "How to Eat the Artichoke"
PANK: "New England Oedipus," "Signs by No Lake That Green"

Ping Pong: "Conjugal Snowscape with Scarecrow"
Pirene's Fountain: "At Edge of Earth, Vacating on the Cheap"
Poem: "Breakthrough"
Porcupine: "Time"
Provincetown Arts magazine: "Wedded"
The Sierra Nevada Review: "Staying with the Mississippi" (reprint)
The Southern Poetry Review: "The Poets"
Spoon River Poetry Review: "Upādāna"
Storyscape Journal: "Staying with the Mississippi"
Terrain.org: "Apocalyptic Swan"
VIA: Voices in Italian Americana: "Metafora"

This manuscript was selected in the Stephen F. Austin State University Press Poetry Series Prize Competition. It was also a 2011-2012 finalist for the Wabash Prize and the Trio House Press Louise Bogan Award, and a semi-finalist for the Wolfson Prize, The Crab Orchard Series Open Competition, and others.

"About Sister" was reprinted in *Token Entry: New York City Subway Poems*, Gerry LaFemina, editor (New York: Smalls Press, 2012).

"At Capri" and "The Eel, Siren" were included in the e-anthology *Eco-Poetry: Poetry of Ecological Sanity*, Daniela Gioseffi, editor (2012).

"Etymology" also appeared on the *Verse Daily* website.

"Tropic Troping Bird" was also featured on the *Wild Violet* website.

Thank you to those editors who nominated these poems for Pushcart Prizes.

My gratitude to many wonderful friends for their sensitive readings of poems in this book: to Sally Dawidoff, about whom I could never say enough; to Lucie Brock-Broido for her luminous spirit, her insight, her passion and dedication, and her support; to Sarah Hannah, my best critic and dear friend, who is still with me in spirit; to David Dodd Lee, whose help made such a difference; to Daniela Gioseffi, *di tutto come sempre;* to Eliza Rotterman, a true lightning gazelle. Heartfelt thanks to Desirée Alvarez, Harry Bauld, Claudia Burbank, Peter Covino, Cynthia Cruz, Lynn Deming, Bergen Hutaff, Harmony Holiday, Rebecca Kutzer-Rice, Helen Klein Ross, Andrew Sage, Jo Sarzotti, Gail Segal, Karen Steinmetz, and Catherine Woodard. Thank you Emily Fragos, friend and poet extraordinaire. Thanks to Rika Lesser, remarkable poet, translator, and healing soul. Thanks to Dean Young, the most amazing person I know. Gratitude to Louise Glück and Larry Raab from my college days; then Stephen

Sandy, Robert Pinksy, Derek Walcott, J. D. McClatchy, Dan Halpern, Mark Rudman, Alice Quinn, and Alfred Corn; and, more recently, Heather McHugh, Robert Hass. Ongoing thanks to my very gifted, insightful, and supportive friends in The Urban Range (www.theurbanrange.com): Ruth Danon, Sally Dawidoff, Elisabeth Frost, David Groff, Melissa Hotchkiss, Hermine Meinhard, and Suzanne Parker. Thanks to my wonderful muse Myra for her continued support, encouragement, and sense of humor. Gratitude to the Napa Valley Writers' Conference and the Squaw Valley Community of Writers for collaboration and community. Thanks to Williams College and the graduate writing programs at Boston University and Columbia University. Thank you, finally, to the team at Stephen F. Austin State University Press for selecting my manuscript. Special gratitude to Kim Verhines, Laura Davis, and Lauren Hawkins for all they have done and do.

ABOUT THE AUTHOR

Stephen Massimilla is a poet, critic, professor, and painter. *The Plague Doctor in His Hull-Shaped Hat* was selected in the 2012 Stephen F. Austin State University Press Poetry Series Prize Competition. Massimilla has received the Bordighera Poetry Prize for his collection *Forty Floors from Yesterday;* the Grolier Prize for *Later on Aiaia;* a Van Rensselaer Award, selected by Kenneth Koch; an Academy of American Poets Prize; and multiple Pushcart Prize nominations. His volume *Almost a Second Thought* was runner-up for the Salmon Run National Poetry Book Award, selected by X. J. Kennedy; and his book *The Happy Tongue* is forthcoming from Tupelo Press. Massimilla has recent poems in *AGNI, American Literary Review, Atlanta Review, Barrow Street, The Bitter Oleander, Chelsea, Colorado Review, Denver Quarterly, Epoch, Green Mountains Review, The Greensboro Review, Provincetown Arts* magazine, *Quarterly West, The Southern Poetry Review, Tampa Review,* and *Verse Daily;* and his poems, essays, and reviews have appeared in hundreds of other journals and anthologies. He is a founding member of The Urban Range poetry collective and holds an M.F.A. and a Ph.D. from Columbia University. Massimilla teaches literary modernism, among other subjects, at Columbia University and the New School. He has also completed hundreds of paintings and thousands of drawings, a portion of which he has exhibited. Visit his website at www.stephenmassimilla.com

CPSIA information can be obtained at www.ICGtesting.com
Printed in the USA
LVOW11s2054130214

373616LV00003B/132/P